Facts About the Great Blue Heron

By Lisa Strattin

© 2016 Lisa Strattin

Revised 2022 © Lisa Strattin

FREE BOOK

FREE FOR ALL SUBSCRIBERS

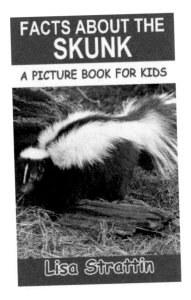

LisaStrattin.com/Subscribe-Here

BOX SET

- **FACTS ABOUT THE POISON DART FROGS**
- **FACTS ABOUT THE THREE TOED SLOTH**
  - **FACTS ABOUT THE RED PANDA**
  - **FACTS ABOUT THE SEAHORSE**
  - **FACTS ABOUT THE PLATYPUS**
  - **FACTS ABOUT THE REINDEER**
  - **FACTS ABOUT THE PANTHER**
- **FACTS ABOUT THE SIBERIAN HUSKY**

LisaStrattin.com/BookBundle

Facts for Kids Picture Books by Lisa Strattin

Little Blue Penguin, Vol 92

Chipmunk, Vol 5

Frilled Lizard, Vol 39

Blue and Gold Macaw, Vol 13

Poison Dart Frogs, Vol 50

Blue Tarantula, Vol 115

African Elephants, Vol 8

Amur Leopard, Vol 89

Sabre Tooth Tiger, Vol 167

Baboon, Vol 174

Sign Up for New Release Emails Here

LisaStrattin.com/subscribe-here

COVER IMAGE

https://www.flickr.com/photos/dapuglet/48349031122/

ADDITIONAL IMAGES

https://www.flickr.com/photos/181920661@N03/51203299518/

https://www.flickr.com/photos/taylar/51940292122/

https://www.flickr.com/photos/21078769@N00/49111167428/

https://www.flickr.com/photos/52450054@N04/46180275924/

https://www.flickr.com/photos/cyclo90/50923510967/

https://www.flickr.com/photos/aly3naa/51835066288/

https://www.flickr.com/photos/132295270@N07/44057557951/

https://www.flickr.com/photos/rosiejuliet/35002579140/

https://www.flickr.com/photos/52450054@N04/51956220010/

https://www.flickr.com/photos/38998067@N04/4356756006/

Contents

INTRODUCTION

The Great Blue Heron belongs to the largest group of birds of North America. They are long legged, fresh water and coastal birds.

They are heavier than Great Egrets but much lighter than the Goliath Heron.

CHARACTERISTICS

The Great Blue Heron are large wading birds found hunting along the coastlines, marshy areas or along fresh water steams, creeks, or rivers. They are superb hunters and can attack their prey with amazing speed.

They take long careful steps while scanning through the water for their prey. They like to wade belly deep in the water.

It's quite a scene to watch them standing motionless for long period before they attack their prey.

APPEARANCE

These are majestic birds. Their flight feathers are grey with a slight navy blue tint on them, with a paler bluish-colored head. Their neck is a rusty grey. They have long feathers below their neck. The back of the head to just above the eyes is covered with a black or grey trail.

They have reddish-brown thighs. The yellowish spot on the thighs turns to an orange when the breeding season starts. They usually tuck their heads into an S-shape while flying.

LIFE STAGES

The Great Blue Heron prefer to live and breed in colonies. Adults of the colony migrate to warmer areas of California and Florida during the month of December, then to the cooler areas of Canada during the month of March.

Their colonies can have from five to 500 birds with an average ranging from 150-160 nests. Their living sites are not easily approachable because they are located over high branches.

Their hunting sites are usually 2 ½ miles to 3 miles from their nests. There is one breeding season in each colony and the females choose a new mate every year. Their nests are made of bulky sticks and are large, ranging from 1 ½ feet to 4 feet in width and about 3 feet in depth.

Their nests grow larger year after year. The eggs are pale blue in color. The females usually lay three to six eggs each time in March and April each year. The males take care of incubation, during the daylight hours and the nighttime hours are covered by the females. The eggs hatch after about 27 days.

LIFE SPAN

The average life span of this bird is around 20 years.

SIZE

The average length of a Great Blue Heron ranges from 3 ½ to 4 ½ feet from head to tail. But the average wingspan is about 5 to 6 ½ feet!

The birds weigh between 4 to 8 pounds. While it is just a little smaller than the Great Egret in size, it is twice as heavy.

HABITAT

The Great Blue Heron is native to North America. It mostly lives in Alaska and Canada but migrates in the colder months to warmer climates. Then there are many in the Caribbean, Florida, and Mexico. They do not like frozen water and will stay as near as possible to flowing waters, because it is easier finding fish for food.

DIET

The diet of the Great Blue Heron is mostly fish, but it is an opportunistic feeder. This means that these birds will feed on whatever is presently available.

They are fond of shrimp which they find in the ocean. They also like crabs, small reptiles, and mammals. The herons have long beaks which are straight, so their food slides down its throat.

The beaks are powerful so that they are able to break and kill their food. They also hunt and catch their food by tossing its prey up into the air and then swallowing it whole.

FRIENDS AND ENEMIES

Friends of the Great Blue Herons include buffaloes and rhinos which they like to perch and ride on with ease. These birds have many enemies, mostly some owls, eagles, and hawks.

SUITABILITY AS PETS

The Great Blue Heron is not really a good candidate for a pet. It is a wild species and is not successfully kept as a pet. It is nocturnal and likes to sleep during the day. If you want a bird to be your pet, this is not the one to choose.

COLOR ME

COLOR ME

COLOR ME

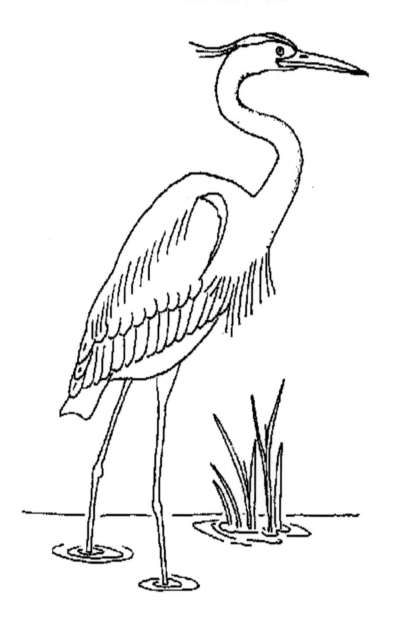

COLOR ME

COLOR ME

COLOR ME

COLOR ME

COLOR ME

COLOR ME

COLOR ME

Please leave me a review here:

LisaStrattin.com/Review-Vol-71

For more Kindle Downloads Visit Lisa Strattin Author Page on Amazon Author Central

amazon.com/author/lisastrattin

To see upcoming titles, visit my website at LisaStrattin.com– most books available on Kindle!

LisaStrattin.com

FREE BOOK

FOR ALL SUBSCRIBERS – SIGN UP NOW

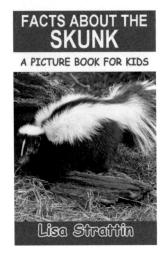

LisaStrattin.com/Subscribe-Here

LisaStrattin.com/Facebook

LisaStrattin.com/Youtube

Made in United States
Troutdale, OR
03/24/2025